W9-BUN-426

A History of American Music

ROCK

Christopher Handyside

Heinemann Library
Chicago, Illinois

Customer Service 888–454–2279
Visit our website at www.heinemannraintree.com

Photo research by Hannah Taylor, Maria Joannou, and Erica Newbery
Designed by Philippa Baile and Ron Kamen
Printed in China by WKT Company Limited

10 09 08 07 06
10 9 8 7 6 5 4 3 2 1

Library of Congress Cataloging-in-Publication Data
Handyside, Chris.
Rock / Christopher Handyside.
p. cm. – (A history of American music)
Includes bibliographical references (p.) and index.
ISBN 1-4034-8152-0 (hc)
1. Rock music–History and criticism–Juvenile literature. I. Title. II.
ML3534.H34 2006
781.66'0973–dc22 2005019307

Acknowledgments
The author and publishers are grateful to the following for permission to reproduce copyright material:
Corbis pp. 16–17 (Jonathan Blair), 30 (Henry Diltz), 37 (Denis O'Regan), 39 (Neal Preston); Getty Images/Hulton Archive p. 5; Redferns pp. 12, 21 (Glen A. Baker), 42 (Mick Hutson), 43 (John Lynn Kirk), 15 (Steve Morley), 32 (Keith Morris), 6, 7, 8, 9, 10, 11, 14, 19, 20, 22, 28–29, 34, 36 (Michael Ochs Archives), 26 (David Redfern), 41 (Ebet Roberts), 31 (Gunter Zint), 23, 41; Redferns/RB p. 40; Redferns/S&G Press Agency p. 25; Sunset Boulevard/Corbis Sygma p. 13; Topham/AP p. 33.

Cover photograph of an electric guitar reproduced with permission of Redferns (Richard Upper).

The publishers would like to thank Patrick Allen for his assistance with the preparation of this book.

Every effort has been made to contact copyright holders of any material reproduced in this book. Any omissions will be rectified in subsequent printings if notice is given to the publishers.

Words shown in **boldface** are defined in the glossary on page 46.

Contents

From Jump to Rock

Rock music is a broad genre of popular music that has its origins in rock and roll (rock 'n' roll). From the mid-1950s through to the 1990s, rock 'n' roll was the most popular form of original American music. From its beginnings as a white offshoot of black rhythm and blues music (R&B), rock 'n' roll has changed with the times. In its early days, rock was a simple mix of country and blues typically played by young men with guitars.

Today, "rock" is an umbrella term for dozens of very different styles of music. However, all are characterized by the central use of electric guitars, an energetic and passionate vocal style, and a backbeat provided by (usually) the snare drum. At its heart, rock music is for young people. It is also the music of rebellion, so it must change to keep up with the times.

The source of rock music is in the 1940s R&B sound that was wildly popular among African-American audiences in the South, and in major cities in the North. Musicians such as R&B **jump-blues** bandleader Louis Jordan had a significant impact on rock 'n' roll's development. Jump blues used a large band, typically with a stand-up bass and a horn section (with saxophones, trombones, and trumpets). It was played much faster than regular blues, and was meant for dancing. The records these artists made were called "race" records, because they were intended for a black audience. However, a lot of white people enjoyed them as well.

Country was also an important influence on the early development of rock 'n' roll. In Memphis, Tennessee, radio stations such as WDIA were playing black R&B, blues, and gospel, as well as white country music, for mixed audiences. This was the perfect melting pot of music and led to the birth of rock 'n' roll. It is difficult to say exactly what the first rock 'n' roll song was. Since rock evolved from country and R&B, many songs with some of the sounds of rock 'n' roll came along before 1954.

Bill Haley and his Comets. Bill Haley is second from right.

In 1952, a piano player, singer, and bandleader from Pennsylvania named Bill Haley and his group, the Saddlemen (who later changed their name to the Comets), released a **cover** version of a Jackie Brenston and Ike Turner R&B song from 1951, called "Rocket 88." This boastful song about the singer's car featured a fast, driving beat, a catchy piano melody, and a chugging rhythm played by the bass, piano, and horns. Like other R&B songs, it was easy to dance to. Haley added a bit of country music guitar flavor to the song, but changed little else.

Many people thought that Jackie Brenston and the Kings of Rhythm's "Rocket 88" was the first rock 'n' roll record, but Haley's version crossed over to white audiences, introducing them to the R&B sound. In 1953, Haley followed it up with the song "Crazy Man Crazy," which became the first rock song by a white performer to hit the American charts.

Another pioneering rock 'n' roll record was Elvis Presley's 1954 recording "That's All Right." When Presley recorded it, music was in a state of change. Presley combined just the right elements of country music, blues, and R&B. He also added his own charisma and attitude to the music—and rock 'n' roll is as much about attitude as it is about musical structure. In 1955, Elvis Presley was still best known regionally in the South. He did not become popular nationally until 1956, but he was still on the leading edge of rock 'n' roll.

Jackie Brenston, one of the founding fathers of rock 'n' roll.

Elvis Presley performing on stage in 1954.

Early Rockers

After the release of Haley and Presley's records, rock 'n' roll quickly gathered pace. In several parts of the country, rock's pioneers were drawing crowds and making groundbreaking records. Most of them had been playing rock 'n' roll in some form before the genre even had a name. In Chicago, Chuck Berry cranked out hits from 1955 through the early 1960s. His songs were heavily influenced by the jump blues of Louis Jordan, but instead of piano and horns, Berry used piano and guitar. His mix of blues and country playing, with his amplifier turned up loud, was not just inventive, but thrilling for 1950s listeners.

Berry became a rock 'n' roll star by writing songs about everyday teenage America. He recorded songs about school ("School Days"), teenage romance ("Sweet Little Sixteen"), and driving around in cars ("No Particular Place To Go"). With his first hit, "Maybellene," Berry actually wrote about all three in the same song.

During his exciting live shows, he played guitar solos while squatting down to the ground, kicking his leg out, and moving across the stage. He called this the "Duck Walk" and it became his trademark stage move. His wild performances, and his slick looks and style, made Chuck Berry extremely popular with young audiences in the 1950s.

Chuck Berry—doing the "Duck Walk." Berry's exciting guitar style has been widely imitated.

Richard Penniman, better known as Little Richard, was even more wild and outrageous on stage than Chuck Berry. Little Richard had a tall, crazy hairstyle, he pounded on the piano like it was a drum, and shouted out his songs like a Southern gospel preacher. He sang phrases such as *"A wop-bop-a-loo-bop/a-lop-bam-boom"*, which confused and frightened parents who didn't know what they meant! However, the real impact of Little Richard was his live performances. He would start by sitting behind his piano. By the end of the song he was standing, stomping, shouting, and working the audience into a frenzy.

Little Richard (on piano) performing live wih his band in the 1950s.

A white musician similar in style to Little Richard was Jerry Lee Lewis from Ferriday, Louisiana. Lewis also played the piano and had a crazy hairstyle. Lewis banged on the piano, sang like a country boy, and was loud and irresistible. In live performances, Lewis often bashed out his piano part with his feet, occasionally lighting the keys on fire. His major hit song was called "Great Balls of Fire."

By the mid-1950s, **rockabilly** was emerging as a popular style. This was an up-tempo mixture of country and R&B music, as performed and recorded by Elvis Presley and Jerry Lee Lewis. Artists such as bespectacled Texan Buddy Holly took rockabilly in a more parent-friendly pop direction with his sweet, catchy songs "Peggy Sue" and "Rave On." However, in 1959, just as Holly's popularity was growing, he died in a plane crash near Clear Lake, Iowa with two other early rock 'n' roll stars, The Big Bopper and Richie Valens.

Buddy Holly's look and style were imitated by artists such as Elvis Costello and David Byrne in the late 1970s and 1980s.

Other major early rock 'n' roll stars included New Orleans piano player Antoine "Fats" Domino, who had popular hits with the slow-dance song "Blueberry Hill" and the more upbeat "I'm Walkin'." Another architect of rock 'n' roll was Bo Diddley, a Mississippi-born former boxer who created a blues style all his own in the early 1950s. With his custom-made rectangular-shaped guitars and his rhythmic, scratching guitar-playing style, Diddley would have gotten attention even without his outlandish clothing and thick, black-framed glasses. He also constantly referred to himself in the third person. Diddley was a strange sight, but it was his sound that made him famous. His songs "Hey, Bo Diddley" and "Who Do You Love?" may not have been as popular as Berry's, but they brought a strange charm to early rock 'n' roll.

Bo Diddley's emphasis on rhythm had a big impact on the rock 'n' roll sound of the 1960s.

Elvis: The King

Even if Elvis did not single-handedly invent rock 'n' roll, he was certainly responsible for its massive popularity. The future King of Rock 'n' Roll was born in Tupelo, Mississippi, on January 8, 1935. His parents moved to Memphis when Presley was a young teenager. Even though he was a kid from the country, Elvis loved more than just country music. In Memphis, he listened to R&B singer Rufus Thomas' show on the WDIA radio station. Thomas played blues, R&B, country, bluegrass, and gospel, and Elvis liked it all. His first love was the country and gospel music he heard around the house. But the music that inspired him when he popularized rock 'n' roll was the African-American blues and R&B he was hearing in Memphis.

In 1954, Elvis went to the studio of Sam Phillips (later named Sun Studio) to make a record for his mother as a birthday present. At that time, Elvis was just a teenager working as a truck driver. Phillips realized that Presley had a great singing voice. More than that, Elvis shared Phillips' color-blind love for American music—country, gospel, and blues. Phillips picked Bill Black, a double bass player, and Scotty Moore, a guitarist, from a local country act to play backup on Elvis's songs. The trio recorded a version of blues artist Big Boy Crudup's "That's All Right" and bluegrass legend Bill Monroe's "Blue Moon of Kentucky."

Sam Phillips (far right) in his recording studio with Elvis (left) and his backing group, Scotty Moore (center) and Bill Black (right).

After "That's All Right" secured his place as a recording artist, Sun Studio sent Elvis out on the road with Moore and Black as a three-piece group. Elvis's electrifying live performances quickly gained the trio a loyal following in the South. His dancing also caught the attention of both his teen fans and their parents. At a time when pop singers were content to just sing on stage, Presley's wild hip-swiveling dance moves, longer hair, and rebellious attitude soon got him noticed. In his performances on such radio shows as the *Louisiana Hayride*, Elvis overshadowed even the most popular Nashville country artists of the time.

Elvis' hip-swiveling greatly worried the parents of his teen fans!

Sam Phillips and Sun Studio

The one thing that two of rock's earliest landmark recordings have in common is one man: Sam Phillips. In 1950, Phillips opened his Memphis Recording Service. Its motto was "We Record Anything–Anywhere–Anytime." Phillips believed that it was the music that mattered, not the color of the musician's skin. "That's All Right" and the original "Rocket 88" were both recorded by the Memphis producer.

Sam Phillips also recorded early songs by future rockabilly and country star Johnny Cash, as well as Carl Perkins, Jerry Lee Lewis, and Roy Orbison. Phillips paid the bills by recording everything from country & western to the occasional song by a random local person who just wanted to make a record for the fun of it. As it turned out, Elvis was one of those locals.

The Comeback

In 1968, Elvis staged an elaborate "comeback special" performance on national television. He performed many of his old hits with newfound energy, looking great in a black leather outfit. The success of this special show inspired him to return to concert performances full-time. Elvis was booked for extended engagements in Las Vegas and was once again a top concert draw.

Most of the songs that established Elvis Presley as a hit maker had already been recorded by other, usually black, artists. It was testament to Elvis's wide-ranging love of American music from both black and white culture that he could translate the passion of the originals to a mainstream, white audience. In fact, Elvis often made them more exciting, just by performing them with his trademark, sneering, hip-swiveling attitude.

Many people viewed this as stealing. The original artists often received no money, while Elvis sold millions of copies of songs such as "Mystery Train." However, some people thought Elvis was actually helping out the original artists, by giving them exposure that they never would have had otherwise.

In 1956, Sun owner Sam Phillips was looking for cash to keep his label afloat. He sold Elvis's recording contract to major label RCA for $35,000. This helped Phillips expand Sun Records. At the same time, Elvis found a new manager, Colonel Tom Parker. At RCA, Presley continued making hits with songs such as "Heartbreak Hotel," "All Shook Up," and "Hound Dog." RCA had the money and resources to introduce Presley to a larger audience. They spent more money on recording and focused on releasing records for a popular audience. These had a cleaner, less raw sound.

In 1956, Presley made the first of three appearances on national television's *The Ed Sullivan Show*. He then spent the end of the 1950s in the U.S. army. He later resumed his career by acting in and recording the soundtrack to a number of generally forgettable films. After his 1968 comeback (see sidebar), Elvis slowly altered his image into that of a Las Vegas showroom performer. However, behind the scenes he was battling with obesity and an increasing dependency on prescription drugs. Elvis Presley died on August 16, 1977, aged just 42.

Elvis in Las Vegas mode in 1976, the year before his death.

Surf's Up!

In the late 1950s, rockabilly was the most popular form of rock 'n' roll. It was a national craze that eventually found its way to the West Coast. In California, a budding guitar player named Dick Dale began to redefine the sound of rock 'n' roll in an entirely new way by inventing "surf music." Surf music became one of the last new American rock 'n' roll styles to achieve mass popularity, before the Beatles and the so-called "British Invasion" took over popular music in 1964.

Dale was an avid surfer and, in 1960, he struck upon the idea of guitar-based instrumental music that tried to create the feelings and sounds he felt while surfing. Dale's guitar sound consisted of plucking the strings individually and very fast with large amounts of **reverb**—an echo effect made when played through an amplifier. He played this frantic style over a driving beat.

Dale worked with a band named the Del-Tones. His guitar melodies were influenced by the Middle Eastern and eastern European folk music that he had heard as a child (his father was Lebanese and his mother was Polish). This turned out to be not only a revolutionary mix of sounds, but also very popular with his surfing buddies. The style quickly caught on with thousands of California kids.

In 1961, Dale recorded and released the first "surf" record, "Let's Go Trippin." Soon after, he released the definitive surf single, "Misirlou." The single was a frantic, charging song that accomplished Dale's goal of describing surfing through music. Dale's influence on rock 'n' roll—and surf music in particular—was also felt in his loud, wild live shows. He often broke many of his guitar strings and went through dozens of picks during a show. He also played louder than anyone had heard rock music played before.

Following Dale's success, many instrumental surf bands, such as the Surfaris, the Ventures, and the Trashmen, formed. They achieved fame nationwide, with hits such as the Surfaris' classic "Wipe Out." Dale himself remained popular through the mid-1960s and enjoyed a successful comeback in 1994, when "Misirlou" was used by filmmaker Quentin Tarantino as the theme song for his hit film *Pulp Fiction*.

Surfing had become extremely popular with California teenagers during the late 1950s and early 1960s.

The Beach Boys

As surfing and surf music became popular, groups that mixed pop vocals with the surfing attitude and sound also became popular. The most successful of these was the Beach Boys.

The Beach Boys were formed in 1961, around the trio of brothers Brian, Carl, and Dennis Wilson, their cousin, Mike Love, and school friend, Al Jardine. Growing up, the Wilsons loved pop vocal groups, such as the Four Freshmen, and they closely studied their vocal style. The leader of the group was Brian, a budding musical genius. But it was the youngest Wilson brother, Dennis, who gave the band their cultural connection. He was a surfer and would return home from a day of surfing with tales of the unique culture that was growing in popularity on the beach. So the Beach Boys were born—a **hybrid** of tight vocal **harmonies**, lyrics about the beach, surfing, and cars, and music that emphasized "reverb" guitar.

The Beach Boys soon broke out of the local California scene when they scored nationwide hits with "Surfin' U.S.A." and "Surfin' Safari," in 1962. Even though Dale was the first surf rocker, the Beach Boys were much more popular because they were singers. This made them more accessible than Dale, who was strictly an instrumental artist. The Beach Boys also continued to change shifts in the youth culture. When the surfing craze began to fade, Brian Wilson led the Beach Boys into new musical territory. His skills in the recording studio were growing quickly, and he was able to capture the sounds he heard in his imagination. This push for growth resulted in grand and overwhelming pop rock 'n' roll, such as the classic single "Good Vibrations."

The Beach Boys continued to enjoy growing artistic achievements and popular success until the late 1960s, when Brian Wilson began suffering mental breakdowns. He withdrew from performances with the band in 1964, but Wilson's innovative songwriting and studio work had a great deal of influence on the English band that soon changed popular rock 'n' roll forever— the Beatles.

The Beach Boys photographed in 1962. The band's 1966 album Pet Sounds *was the first so-called* ***concept album****.*

Girl Groups

The other major pop music trend that sprung up between the birth of rock 'n' roll in the 1950s and the British Invasion of the mid-1960s was the girl group. Early groups, such as the Shirelles, became popular in the late 1950s as an outgrowth of the vocal pop style known as **doo-wop**, mixed with a smooth R&B-influenced style. To this mix, the girl groups added style, grace, and a kind of romantic innocence to their singing. The Shirelles formed while the members were still in high school in New Jersey, in 1958. They had a huge hit in 1961 with "Will You Still Love Me Tomorrow?"

Following on the heels of the Shirelles' success, The Shangri-Las were a very popular girl group. The quartet, who later became a trio, formed in 1963. They were attractive, tough-looking women, decked out in mini-skirts and leather knee-high boots, and sang beautiful and sad songs. Their biggest hit was 1964's "Leader of the Pack." The song told the story of a woman's motorcycle-gang leader boyfriend who dies in a crash. They took the polished singing style of the Shirelles and added a bit of a rock 'n' roll "bad-girl" attitude.

The members of The Shangri-Las were only 16 years old when they recorded their smash hit "Leader of the Pack."

The Wall of Sound

Besides the Shangri-Las, two other popular girl groups were the Crystals and the Ronettes. Both groups had one thing in common: producer, songwriter, and label boss Phil Spector put them together. Spector was one of the most influential of all rock 'n' roll music producers (see sidebar). The Ronettes were a trio of young New York women fronted by the powerful-voiced lead singer, Ronnie Bennett. Their biggest hit, "Be My Baby" in 1963, was one of the most popular songs from a girl group and featured not just Bennett's romantic, impassioned vocals, but Spector's famous "Wall of Sound" production. This included an intricate mix of strings, harmonies, and percussion instruments, which created a beautiful, rich, and powerful sound.

The influence of Phil Spector's Wall of Sound was felt far beyond the girl group phenomenon. Besides Spector's later work with such bands as the Beatles, punk group the Ramones, and many others, the Wall of Sound approach was a direct inspiration for such well known producers as Andrew Loog Oldham, who worked with the Rolling Stones. Spector also greatly influenced the Beach Boys' Brian Wilson. Wilson was so inspired by the Ronettes', "Be My Baby," he wrote a response song called "Don't Worry Baby" in the same style. Spector rejected it as a Ronettes' song, but the Beach Boys recorded it in 1964, and "Don't Worry Baby" became a huge hit.

Phil Spector with the Ronettes in the 1960s.

The British Invasion: The UK is Listening

Meanwhile, across the Atlantic Ocean, young people were getting into this new American music. Records by Elvis Presley, Chuck Berry, Buddy Holly, and Bo Diddley made their way to British music fans. In Britain, records by African Americans were not segregated as "race records." Rock 'n' roll, blues, and R&B records were all sold together and British kids heard an exciting melting pot of sounds coming from the United States. Many decided to form rock bands of their own.

The "British Invasion" of the United States took place in 1964. It was led by groups such as the Beatles, the Rolling Stones, and the Who, and it altered the rules of rock 'n' roll forever. Before the British Invasion, many pop stars and rock 'n' rollers such as Elvis Presley, the 1960s girl groups, and many of the stars from the pop-soul label Motown only performed songs written by other people. Chuck Berry, the Beach Boys, and Buddy Holly were notable exceptions to this rule.

The Who in 1964. The band were an important part of the British Invasion.

The Beatles

In 1957, in Liverpool, a group of young men started experimenting. They combined early rock 'n' roll from artists like Buddy Holly and Chuck Berry with the polished pop R&B sound of groups such as the Supremes from the Motown label. John Lennon, Paul McCartney, and George Harrison of the Beatles were not the only band in the Liverpool area to attempt this mix of influences. But they were soon acknowledged as the best of the bunch.

John Lennon and Paul McCartney played together from 1957 in a band called the Quarrymen. They were inspired by the early rockabilly of Elvis Presley and Carl Perkins. By 1960, they had changed their name to the Beatles and had added guitarist George Harrison and drummer Pete Best to the group. The Beatles perfected their energetic live performance by playing rock 'n' roll cover songs for audiences in rundown clubs in Hamburg, Germany. They returned to Liverpool in 1962. The night before their first recording session, the band replaced drummer Pete Best with Ringo Starr. That recording session resulted in the release of the band's first UK single, "Love Me Do" and "P.S. I Love You." Both of these songs were co-credited to Lennon and McCartney.

The group's sound had come together. The dual guitars of Lennon and Harrison, the propulsive rhythm of Starr and McCartney, and the quartet's sweet vocal harmonies and enthusiastic delivery of such songs as "She Loves You (Yeah, Yeah, Yeah)" drove the fans wild.

The Beatles on stage in 1963.

In December 1963, the Beatles released the romantic, but upbeat, "She Loves You" and "I Want to Hold Your Hand" as their first U.S. singles. Music fans went crazy for them. "I Want to Hold Your Hand" was an instant number-one hit song. In February 1964, the Beatles came to the United States for the first time to appear on the *The Ed Sullivan Show.* So many fans flocked to New York City's JFK Airport that the screaming was deafening. Over the next two years, the Beatles toured extensively throughout the world.

The Beatles provided a fresh, exciting, and sometimes experimental approach to rock, with a very strong emphasis on melody. By 1965, they had evolved their original sound to include folk-influenced guitar parts and poetic, thoughtful lyrics very different from the innocence of "I Want To Hold Your Hand." That year's album, *Rubber Soul*, influenced the folk-rock movement in the United States, particularly bands such as the Byrds.

In 1966, the Beatles outdid themselves with their incredibly influential **psychedelic** breakthrough album *Revolver*. It featured swirling guitar, pounding percussion, and studio trickery on some songs, as well as straight rock 'n' roll numbers. This album became a major influence on the developing San Francisco rock scene and bands like Jefferson Airplane.

The Beatles returned in 1967 with their concept album, *Sgt. Pepper's Lonely Hearts Club Band*, a record that mixed rock 'n' roll with old-fashioned songs. In with the rock 'n' roll, they threw in bits of classical music and anything else that had inspired them. It was a **landmark** record that inspired many American artists.

The Beatles broke up on April 10, 1970. In seven years they did more to expand the sound of rock 'n' roll music than any other band before or since. While there is no doubt that rock 'n' roll started in the United States, the Beatles were responsible for showing just how much it could be developed.

Beatles arriving at New York City's JFK Airport in 1964.

The Rolling Stones at Chess Studios in 1964.

The Rolling Stones

During roughly the same time period as the Beatles' sound was invading the U.S., a London-based quintet named The Rolling Stones were busy exploring a path that had even stronger links to American blues music. The core trio of singer Mick Jagger, guitarist Keith Richards, and multi-instrumentalist Brian Jones performed songs by blues artists Howlin' Wolf, Muddy Waters, Chuck Berry, and other rock 'n' rollers. By the time of their record debut in 1963, the Stones were seen as the rebellious alternative to the squeaky-clean Beatles.

The Rolling Stones scored their first American chart hit in 1964 with a leering cover of "Not Fade Away" by Buddy Holly. They first visited the United States in the summer of 1964 and joined in the British Invasion. While there, they paid tribute to their U.S. influences by visiting Chess Records, the home of the blues in Chicago, where they recorded a five-song record.

"The Stones" may have been seen as the bad boys of the British Invasion, but as they evolved they experimented with some of the same ideas as their competition. They became one of the first bands to play truly hard rock. Interestingly, in the late 1960s they moved into country-rock, directly influenced by the American country singer-songwriter Gram Parsons. But even as they experimented, The Stones continued to release hard-rock songs such as the 1968 hit "Jumpin' Jack Flash."

The Rolling Stones reintroduced U.S. musicians to the blues roots of rock, and paved the way for the hard rock and heavy metal sounds of the late 1960s through to the 1980s. The group's original lineup stayed together until Jones was kicked out of the band in June 1969. He was found dead less than a month later, drowned in his swimming pool. The band eventually settled into a comfortable career as "the Greatest Rock Band in the World," touring around the globe.

The Ed Sullivan Show

The CBS television program *The Ed Sullivan Show* played a major role in introducing the Beatles and most of the other British Invasion bands to the United States. This variety show featured comedians, singers, dancers, and skits. At the time, it was one of the most popular shows on television.

Despite the show's tendency toward tame entertainment, it was the first show to feature many rock 'n' rollers, including Elvis Presley. When the Beatles were first beamed into American living rooms playing live, the impact was huge.

Over the next few years, the Beatles made a number of appearances on the show, as did the Rolling Stones, the Who, and other British Invasion bands.

Psych Out

The mid-1960s were a time of great political and social upheaval. The Civil Rights movement seeking equal rights for African Americans had succeeded with President Lyndon Johnson's signing of the **Civil Rights Act** in 1964. The acceptance of blacks by many young, white Americans was, at least in part, brought on by the culturally and racially diverse stars of rock 'n' roll. In the late 1960s, when the United States became more and more involved in the conflict in Vietnam, folk-rock artists, such as Bob Dylan and the Byrds, provided the soundtrack to mass **protests**.

The new psychedelic sound that developed in the mid-1960s differed from the rock 'n' roll that had come before in several ways. First, the Byrds, the Beatles, and others began playing songs longer than the three-minute rock 'n' roll formula, often featuring instrumental solos. They also started to experiment with studio effects that altered the sound of their instruments. Finally, their songs were about deeper subjects, such as the nature of the mind, the universe, and social problems. Psych rock, and the folk-rock from which it grew, sought to promote racial and cultural diversity. Artists participated in Civil Rights struggles, sang about harmony and tolerance, and embraced music styles from around the world.

The hotspot for the psychedelic movement was the West Coast. In San Francisco, dozens of bands formed and lived in and around the Haight-Asbury neighborhood. These bands and their fans and neighbors became known as hippies. The hippie community believed that they could change the world through the arts, spiritual freedom, and acceptance of others.

One of the first hippie bands was Jefferson Airplane. Their 1967 album *Surrealistic Pillow* featured two defining songs of the genre. The first, "Somebody to Love," introduced the world to the powerful voice of Grace Slick. The next was "White Rabbit," a slower song with a Spanish-influenced rhythm and lyrics inspired by Lewis Carroll's story *Alice's Adventures in Wonderland*. Bands in the area were also creating innovative music, rooted in country, folk, and blues and mixed with rock 'n' roll. Others included the Mamas and Papas, the Lovin' Spoonful, the improvisation-heavy band the Grateful Dead, and blues-rock singing sensation Janis Joplin. As these bands became popular, the hippie movement spread across the country.

In June 1967, tens of thousands of hippies and music fans gathered in Monterey, California, for the Monterey International Pop Festival. This became a legendary event and a key moment in hippie history. Jefferson Airplane, Joplin, Jimi Hendrix, and British hard-rockers the Who, all played definitive sets.

Jefferson Airplane performing in 1967.

Jimi Hendrix

Before Monterey, Jimi Hendrix had been building an ever-growing fan base for his groundbreaking guitar playing. He based his style in the R&B that he regularly played as a backing musician on tours throughout the early 1960s. He was also influenced by the loud and wild playing of surf guitar innovator Dick Dale. By the mid-1960s, Hendrix had created a style of guitar playing that has influenced generations of guitarists. He first perfected his freeform, fiery style playing for audiences in the UK. American audiences were not yet ready to accept his innovative and creative technique.

Only after Hendrix became wildly popular in Britain was he accepted in his homeland. But after setting fire to his guitar at Monterey, Hendrix became one of the biggest names in rock 'n' roll. His version of Bob Dylan's "All Along the Watchtower" and hits such as "Hey Joe" and "Purple Haze" are rock classics and perfect examples of psych rock.

Jimi Hendrix playing at Woodstock in 1969.

Jim Morrison and The Doors

The defining moment in 1960s rock 'n' roll was the Woodstock Music and Art Fair held at Bethel, New York, on August 15–17, 1969. Now known simply as "Woodstock", the festival brought together the biggest names in rock music with an estimated 500,000 fans for a weekend of peace, love, and music. Janis Joplin, the Grateful Dead, Creedence Clearwater Revival, Jefferson Airplane, Jimi Hendrix, and dozens of others performed. The festival was not without problems. Roads backed up for miles leading to the site, so fans just parked and walked. On the first day the gates at the site were knocked down by concertgoers and Woodstock became essentially a free concert! On the last day of Woodstock, weary fans greeted the day with Jimi Hendrix playing his famous solo-guitar rendition of the "Star Spangled Banner."

Down the coast from San Francisco, a quartet called The Doors were making waves on the Los Angeles music scene with their combination of poetry and **improvised** rock 'n' roll. The Doors' sound was based around the organ playing of Ray Manzarek, a rich, swirling sound that recalled Indian, R&B, jazz, and classical music influences. But it was singer Jim Morrison's poetic lyrics, deep voice, and larger-than-life stage persona that became the symbol of The Doors. Morrison's lyrics dealt with big, sometimes dark issues such as life, death, consciousness, and love. The Doors released their self-titled debut album in 1967 and their first single "Light My Fire," was a massive hit. It was followed by the dark song "Break On Through (To The Other Side)."

Jim Morrison (left) and The Doors in 1968.

The End of an Era

The upbeat, positive spirit of the 1960s ended in the early 1970s with the high profile deaths of three of its brightest stars—Jimi Hendrix, Jim Morrison, and Janis Joplin. All three died of drug and alcohol abuse.

This was a wake-up call to the dangerous consequences of the rock 'n' roll lifestyle. The peace and love feeling of the times had already started to come unglued with three political events in 1968. The first was the assassination of African-American Civil Rights leader Martin Luther King Jr. The second was the assassination of presidential candidate (and late President John F. Kennedy's younger brother) Robert Kennedy. The third was the rioting and violence at the 1968 **Democratic National Convention** in Chicago. During the outdoor performance of Detroit political rock band the MC5, Chicago police tried to break up the show and viciously clubbed many of the fans and political activists.

After her death in 1970, Janis Joplin was crowned "Queen of the Blues" by devoted fans.

The Rolling Stones performing at the troubled Altamont Festival in 1969.

However, the most significant event to signal the end of the 1960s era was the Altamont Festival in Livermore, California on December 6, 1969. The free, all-day show was billed as a sort of Woodstock of the West. The Rolling Stones, Jefferson Airplane, and the Grateful Dead played. Instead of the peace and love feeling of the Monterey International Pop or Woodstock festivals, Altamont was tense, gloomy, and tragic. The notorious motorcycle gang, the Hell's Angels, provided security for the event and spent much of the day bullying and attacking members of the crowd. During the Rolling Stones' set, a fight broke out between a member of the Hell's Angels and concertgoer Meredith Hunter. Hunter was killed. The 1960s were over, both literally and symbolically.

A Heavier Sound

Even before the passing of Hendrix, Joplin, and Morrison, there were rumblings in the musical underground that pointed in a new direction. The late 1960s were a turbulent period in American history, with urban riots in cities, including Los Angeles and Detroit. Protests over the Vietnam War resulted in young people turning more toward anger and away from the peace and love the hippies had preached about.

One of the first bands to recognize the mood and express it musically was the New York quartet the Velvet Underground. Formed in the mid-1960s around the songwriting duo of young lyricist Lou Reed and Welsh experimental musician John Cale, the Velvet Underground wrote songs that reflected the harsh, everyday life in New York City.

The Velvet Underground, (from left to right) Sterling Morrison, Lou Reed, Mo Tucker, and John Cale.

Reed had started in the music business attempting to write pop songs for other artists, but he really found his voice when he focused on the darker side of life. Reed's half-spoken, half-sung vocal delivery broke from conventional rock 'n' roll style and inspired many other songwriters whose voices were less "pop-friendly" to sing. Other trademark sounds of the Velvet Underground were Cale's moody use of cello, viola, and non-traditional rock instruments. Guitarist Sterling Morrison and drummer Maureen "Mo" Tucker provided a steady, ultra-basic rhythm, mostly playing on only one thumping drum. The band's sometimes vocalist was Nico, a German artist and model whose low, heavily-accented voice provided an exotic counterpoint to Reed's straightforward lyrical reading.

The Velvet Underground recorded only four albums in their brief career and none of them sold well. Even so, the band influenced many musicians, especially those in New York's rock 'n' roll and developing **punk rock** scenes.

At about the same time, a group of men from a working class suburb of Detroit formed the Motor City 5. The group shared a love of British R&B and American soul music. By the time they shortened their name to the MC5, they were also exploring the noisy, freeform improvisational sounds of avant-garde jazz. They played legendary shows at Detroit's Grande Ballroom. Guitarists Fred "Sonic" Smith and Wayne Kramer created some of the most heavy, intense rock 'n' roll guitar sounds ever heard. Front man Rob Tyner was a powerfully soulful singer. They fused the sweaty energy of soul and rock music with the intense politics of the day, and played it all at ear-splitting volume.

By 1972, MC5 had been through too many legal and personal problems to continue, and they played their last gig on New Year's Eve 1972. They left behind a recording and performance legacy that helped to inspire punk rock. More immediately, their popularity supported a creative rock scene that helped give birth to other heavy bands.

At the end of the 1960s, one band took the prevailing mood of hopelessness one step further, and down a more shocking path. In 1969, in Ann Arbor, Michigan, a former drummer named James Osterberg changed his name to Iggy Stooge (later, Iggy Pop) and founded the hard rock band, the Stooges.

The Stooges included two brothers, Ron and Scott Asheton, who played guitar and drums. The Stooges' sound was loud, heavy, and crushingly repetitive. Iggy sang songs of alienation and despair. "I Wanna Be Your Dog" and "1969" showed a new approach to rock 'n' roll that had nothing to do with the peace and love of the 1960s—except to affirm that it had ended and kids were fed up. When the band played live, Iggy Pop provided a wild, visual spectacle for the audience.

Iggy Pop (front left) with the Stooges and Lou Reed (top left).

An even more theatrical spectacle was created by another artist with Michigan ties. Alice Cooper was directly inspired by bands such as the Stooges, and the British music style known as "**glam rock**." Cooper pioneered what was called horror-rock (or shock rock) by adding a level of haunted-house theatrics to his performances. His show included live snakes, guillotines—complete with staged "beheadings"—and other gruesome sights. Cooper's hit songs, such as "Welcome to My Nightmare" and "No More Mr. Nice Guy," fit this dark mood. Cooper dressed up as a sort of undead ringmaster, complete with black eye-makeup, pale face, top hat, tails, and a cane.

Alice Cooper in the 1970s, performing with a live snake.

Led Zeppelin, AOR, and Heavy Metal

Led Zeppelin's first two albums, *Led Zeppelin* and *Led Zeppelin II*, were both released in 1969. They were huge hits not just in their native Britain, but also in the United States. With these two heavy rock albums, Zeppelin changed the way music was sold. Before Zeppelin, it was standard practice for a band to release "singles." Singles are songs selected especially to play on the radio. Led Zeppelin did not release singles. They simply released the albums and left it up to radio DJs to pick what song they were going to play. By ditching the singles, Led Zeppelin put emphasis on the whole album as the work of art.

The Beatles, the Rolling Stones, the Beach Boys, and The Doors had already produced collections of songs meant to be played together (albums) for maximum artistic effect. However, these bands still released the catchier singles off of their albums. Zeppelin's new approach was called Album-Oriented Rock (or AOR). It became standard practice in the 1970s among the hard rock and heavy metal bands that were inspired by Led Zeppelin. When the seven minute-long Zeppelin song "Stairway to Heaven" became a huge hit, it was because DJs actually liked it and listeners requested it.

Other British bands such as Black Sabbath and Deep Purple helped to lay the foundations of heavy metal rock. In 1974, the U.S. heavy metal band KISS burst upon the rock scene with their wild costumes, elaborate face paints and gimmicky live performances. They were to be followed in the 1980s by the enormously popular Guns 'N' Roses and the New Jersey rock band Bon Jovi.

Led Zeppelin's Robert Plant (left) and Jimmy Page on stage.

The Zeppelin effect

In the South, musicians such as the Allman Brothers and Lynyrd Skynrd took inspiration from Led Zeppelin, as well as the psychedelic movement. They merged it with old-fashioned country to create a unique sound known as "southern rock." Southern rock featured intricate twangy dual guitar lines and rebellious lyrics about skipping town and everyday problems, all sung with pronounced southern accents. Lynyrd Skynyrd's 1973 hits "Sweet Home Alabama" and "Free Bird" are examples of southern rock.

The most notable U.S. band to have formed as a direct result of Led Zeppelin was the Boston quartet Aerosmith. They adopted the flashy dress and attitude—as well as borrowing from and playing the blues in new ways. Front man Steven Tyler and guitarist Joe Perry looked like American versions of Zeppelin's Robert Plant and Jimmy Page. Aerosmith played huge arena shows and rose to the top of the charts with hits such as "Dream On," the rocking "Mama Kin," and the funky "Walk this Way" (which they later remade with rap act RUN-DMC in 1986).

I'm Bored

By the mid-1970s, the adventurous, rebellious rock 'n' roll spirit had been all but extinguished by arena rock. The name derives from the fact that most rock bands on major labels at this time played in huge venues, usually sports arenas, in or near large cities. The energy and excitement generated by seeing a band up-close and personal was now missing. As a reaction against the stagnant AOR and massive, money-generating rock shows, the punk rock movement of the 1970s was born.

The New York musicians and fans that hung around clubs, such as CBGBs and Max's Kansas City, wanted to make rock that was simple, exciting, and fun. The Ramones and The New York Dolls were two bands responsible for this development.

The New York Dolls formed in 1971 in Manhattan, to mix the flashiness of glam and the simplicity of 1950s and 1960s pop groups, such as The Shangri-Las. But they took it one step further by dressing up in women's clothes and wearing makeup. Their songs, such as "Personality Crisis" and "Lookin' for a Kiss," were fast-paced and bluesy. The New York Dolls were a direct influence on the band that would be called the first "punk" band, the Ramones.

The New York Dolls were punk before punk existed.

The Ramones in the late-1970s.

The Ramones formed in 1974 in the New York City borough of Queens. They loved 1950s rock but could barely play their instruments. Their early songs had the same drumbeat and only three simple guitar chords. However their enthusiasm won them a devoted audience when they started playing live. Their songs began with guitarist Johnny Ramone shouting "1-2-3-4!", followed by two minutes of buzzsaw guitar and nasal, gritty singing.

The Ramones and The New York Dolls both toured England in the mid-1970s, where they had a huge influence. The British reaction to the New York bands came in the form of the Sex Pistols, a loud, disorganized band that sang sneering songs about the Queen of England and running wild in the streets. Another major band on the London punk scene was the Clash. The Clash were less gritty than the Sex Pistols, but the music on their first, self-titled album from 1977 was clearly influenced by The Ramones.

By the time the Sex Pistols and the Clash got a hold of punk rock, it was a large youth movement in England It soon became a popular music and fashion statement among young Americans, too. The New York punk scene in the 1970s saw the rise of important bands such as Blondie and the Talking Heads. In both countries punk rock had more of a cultural than commercial impact. Punk culture inspired kids to start their own bands because musical skill was less important than confidence, opinions, enthusiasm, and energy.

Smells Like Grunge

Throughout the 1980s, rock 'n' roll innovation seemed to have come to a standstill. Pop-metal bands such as Motley Crue, Bon Jovi, Poison, Ratt, and others often seemed to be more interested in hairstyles and tight leather clothing than musical creativity. The one notable exception were L.A. rockers Guns N' Roses. Their 1987 debut album *Appetite for Destruction* brought the spirit and aggression of punk to their brand of hard rock. Also in 1987 there were rumblings of yet another rock 'n' roll rebirth, coming from the city of Seattle, Washington.

In the small Seattle scene, the bands Mother Love Bone, Mudhoney, the Melvins, and Soundgarden were starting to play music influenced by both the heavy underground punk of the mid-1980s and the heavy-duty sound of 1970s rock bands Black Sabbath and Deep Purple. This music was labeled "grunge."

Kurt Cobain was hailed as a voice of his generation.

The band Nirvana was inspired by these grunge players. Nirvana's Kurt Cobain was a massive Melvins and Mudhoney fan, and by 1989 the band had played enough shows to record and release an album called *Bleach* that had a similar sound. The notable difference was that the songs on *Bleach* were more catchy. Nirvana's second album, *Nevermind*, was released in 1991 with modest expectations. However, the first single "Smells Like Teen Spirit" bumped even Michael Jackson from the top of the charts and ushered in the "grunge era." *Nevermind* was one of the biggest-selling albums of the 1990s.

Nirvana's 1994 album *In Utero* was at times an uncompromising, harsh record and at other times a mellow folk and pop record. Sadly, in April 1994, Kurt Cobain died of a self-inflicted gunshot wound. The success of Nirvana made it possible for the band Pearl Jam to take grunge even further in the direction of pop, with a more polished sound.

Through Grunge the slightly aggressive pop-punk movement gained momentum and produced such bands as Green Day, Rancid, and the Offspring. These bands took the loud, gritty attitude of punk, teamed it with the catchy songwriting tricks of Nirvana, and sold it to a massive audience. Grunge created the template for hundreds of **derivative** bands, such as Creed, Nickelback, the Vines, and others. The guitar and vocal styles, the bleak subject matter, the average-guy fashion sense—it can all be traced back to grunge and Nirvana.

Today in rock, there is the odd breakout of punk-based bands, such as the Yeah Yeah Yeahs and Interpol, and the genre-defying hybrid of The White Stripes' mix of blues, folk, punk, and hard rock. This is clearly an indication that rock 'n' roll will continue to evolve.

Both Green Day and Rancid came from the same do-it-yourself scene. They both started playing in the Berkeley, California punk-rock haven, Gilman Street. At Gilman Street, the bands had to book and promote their own shows, load their own gear, set up their own sound, and often clean up afterward. The humbling experience no doubt led to the perseverance of a band like Green Day even as their fortunes rose, fell, and rose following their multi-platinum 1994 breakthrough, *Dookie*.

Neo-punk bands such as Green Day represent the modern popular face of rock.

Timeline

1619 The first slave ship crosses the Middle Passage of the Atlantic Ocean.

1861–1865 American Civil War. This war between the Union and the Confederacy ended in 1865 with the defeat of the Confederates.

1865 Thirteenth Amendment to the U.S. Constitution abolishes slavery.

1877 Invention of the phonograph by Thomas Edison.

1914–1918 World War I. This war was fought between France, Britain, and the United States against Germany. Germany was defeated in 1918. The United States did not enter the war until 1917.

1920 Commercial radio broadcasting begins in the United States.

1920–1929 The "Roaring Twenties." This decade is also known as the "Jazz Age."

1929 The U.S. Stock Market crash begins the period of the 1930s known as the Great Depression.

1941 The United States enters World War II. The war ends in 1945.

Late 1940s–1973 Period of U.S. involvement in Vietnam. Involvement in Vietnam in the 1960s through 1973 is commonly called the Vietnam War.

1951 Jackie Brenston and his Kings of Rhythm record "Rocket 88," the first rock 'n' roll song.

1954 Elvis Presley records "That's All Right Mama" at Sun Studio, Memphis.

1959 Rock 'n' rollers Buddy Holly, The Big Bopper, and Richie Valens die in a plane crash over Iowa. Motown Records founded in Detroit by Berry Gordy.

1960 The Quarrymen change their name to the Beatles.

1961 Dick Dale invents "surf music" with the single "Let's Go Trippin'."

1962 Pete Seeger writes the song "Turn, Turn, Turn."

1963 Assassination of President John F. Kennedy on November 22nd.
The Ronettes release "Be My Baby" featuring producer Phil Spector's "Wall of Sound."
The Beatles release "I Want to Hold Your Hand" in America.

1964 Civil Rights Act is signed by President Lyndon B. Johnson.
The British Invasion begins.

1965 Bob Dylan plays electric at Newport Folk Festival
Folk-rock band the Byrds form, Los Angeles, CA.

1968 Assassination of African-American Civil Rights leader, Martin Luther King Jr. in April.
Assassination of presidential candidate Robert F. Kennedy, brother of late President John F. Kennedy in June.
Violence erupts in Chicago during demonstrations at the Democratic National Convention in August.

1969 The Woodstock Festival takes place in Bethel, NY.
The Rolling Stones stage the tragic Altamont Festival in Livermore, CA.
Punk innovators the Stooges featuring singer Iggy Pop, release their debut album.

1970 '60s icons Jimi Hendrix, Jim Morrison, and Janis Joplin die.

1974 The Ramones form in Queens, NY.

1991 Seattle rock band Nirvana release their hit record "Nevermind."

Glossary

Civil Rights Act set of laws passed in the United States in 1964 designed to ensure equal protection and rights for African Americans

concept album recordings that have a central theme—either instrumental or via the lyrics

cover when artists record their own, newer version of another artists' music

Democratic National Convention gathering of representatives from the Democratic political party held once every four years to nominate the Democratic candidate for the U.S. presidential election

derivative similar to, or including features of, another work of music

doo-wop form of group vocal music that influenced rock 'n' roll

glam rock style of rock music from the early 1970s that featured flashy fashion, props, and performance style

harmonies sound formed by the combined playing of different tones at the same time

hybrid music that is a combination of different genres

improvise the act of composing and performing, in this case, a piece of music, without preparation

jump blues amplified mixture of up-tempo swing jazz and blues common in urban areas in the 1940s

landmark piece of music that other and future musicians and artists look to for inspiration

protests public demonstration against an activity or thing deemed as unfair

psychedelic term used to describe the hallucinations, vivid colors, and altered state of awareness usually induced by drugs

punk rock a loud, fast-moving, aggressive form of rock music

reverb echo effect produced by the amplifier of an electric guitar

rockabilly mixture of country music and rhythm and blues played by poor, rural white people in the 1950s

Further Information

WEBSITES

Smithsonian Music resources:

www.si.edu/resource/faq/nmah/music.htm

PLACES TO VISIT

Sun Studio, Memphis
706 Union Ave.
Memphis, TN 38103
901-525-8055

Graceland, Memphis
3734 Elvis Presley Blvd.
Memphis, TN 38116
901-332-3322

Experience Music Project
325 5th Ave. N.
Seattle, WA 98109
877-367-5483
www.emplive.org
Huge interactive music museum and archive. Covers all types of popular music—jazz, soul/R&B, rock, country, folk, and blues.

Rock and Roll Hall of Fame Museum
One Key Plaza
751 Erieside Ave
Cleveland, OH 44114
216-781-ROCK
www.rockhall.com
Huge museum that covers not only rock, but folk, country, R&B, blues, and jazz and how all of them have influenced rock over time.

RECORDINGS

Chuck Berry:
The Best of Chuck Berry (Millennium Collection)
(MCA)

Little Richard:
The Essential Little Richard
(Specialty)

The Ronettes:
The Best of the Ronettes
(Abkco)

Beach Boys:
Pet Sounds
(Capitol)

Jefferson Airplane:
Surrealistic Pillow
(RCA)

Jimi Hendrix:
Are You Experienced?
(Experience Hendrix)

Led Zeppelin:
Led Zeppelin (1st)
(Atlantic/WEA)

The Stooges:
Fun House
(Electra/Wea)

Ramones:
Rocket to Russia
(Rhino/Wea)

The Doors:
The Doors
(Electra/Wea)

Aerosmith:
Rocks
(Sony)

Nirvana:
Nevermind
(Geffen Records)

Index

BALDWIN PUBLIC LIBRARY
3 1115 00530 0610